JEANETTE WINTER

WANGARI'S

TREES OF PEACE

A True Story from Africa

HARCOURT, INC.

Orlando   Austin   New York   San Diego   London

Requests for permission to make copies of any part of the work should be submitted online at www.harcourt.com/contact or mailed to the following address: Permissions Department, Harcourt, Inc., 6277 Sea Harbor Drive, Orlando, Florida 32887-6777.

www.HarcourtBooks.com

Library of Congress Cataloging-in-Publication Data
Winter, Jeanette.
Wangari's trees of peace/Jeanette Winter.
p. cm.
1. Maathai, Wangari—Juvenile literature.   2. Tree planters (Persons)—Kenya—Biography—Juvenile literature.   3. Green Belt Movement (Society: Kenya)—Juvenile literature.   4. Women conservationists—Kenya—Biography—Juvenile literature.
5. Women politicians—Kenya—Biography—Juvenile literature.   I. Title.
SB63.M22W56 2008
333.72092—dc22
[B]   2007034810
ISBN 978-0-15-206545-4

TWP 13 12 11 10 9
4500288582

Printed in Singapore

This book was printed on 130gsm Cyclus Print (recycled Matte).
The illustrations in this book were done in acrylic on Arches watercolor paper.
The display lettering was created by Judythe Sieck.
The text type was set in Today Regular.
Color separations by Bright Arts Ltd., Hong Kong
Printed and bound by Tien Wah Press, Singapore
Production supervision by Pascha Gerlinger
Designed by Judythe Sieck

"*The earth was naked.*
For me the mission was to try
to cover it with green."

–WANGARI MAATHAI

Wangari lives under an umbrella of green trees
in the shadow of Mount Kenya in Africa.

She watches the birds in the forest
where she and her mother go to gather
firewood for cooking.

And she helps harvest the sweet potatoes, sugarcane, and maize from the rich soil.

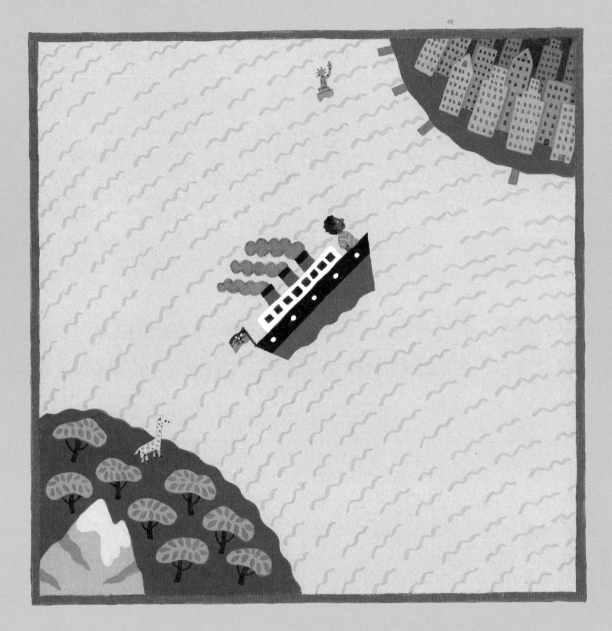

Wangari shines in school,
and when she grows tall, like the trees in the forest,
she wins a scholarship to study in America.

Six years later, her studies over, Wangari returns
to her Kenya home and sees a change.
What has happened? she wonders.
Where are the trees?

Wangari sees women bent from hauling firewood
miles and miles from home.
She sees barren land where no crops grow.
And where are the birds?

Thousands of trees have been cut down to make room
for buildings, but no one planted new trees
to take their place.
Will all of Kenya become a desert? she wonders
as her tears fall.

Wangari thinks about the barren land.
I can begin to replace some of the lost trees
here in my own backyard—one tree at a time.
She starts by planting nine seedlings.

Watching the seedlings take root gives Wangari
the idea to plant more—
to start a farm for baby trees, a nursery.
In an open space, she plants row after row
of the tiny trees.

Next, Wangari convinces the village women
that planting trees is a good thing.
She gives each one a seedling.
"Our lives will be better when we have trees again. You'll see.
We are planting the seeds of hope."

The women spread out over their village,
planting tiny trees in long rows,

like a green belt stretching over the land.

The government men laugh.

"Women can't do this," they say.

"It takes trained foresters to plant trees."

The women ignore the laughter and keep planting.

Wangari pays them a small amount
for each seedling still living after three months—
their first earnings ever.

Word travels, like wind rustling through leaves,
about the green returning to Wangari's village.

Soon other women in other villages and towns and cities in Kenya are planting long rows of seedlings, too.

But the cutting continues.

Wangari stands tall as an oak to protect
the old trees still remaining.
"We need a park more than we need an office tower."

The government men disagree.

Wangari blocks their way, so they hit her with clubs.

They call her a troublemaker and put her in jail.

And still she stands tall.

Right is right, even if you're alone.

But Wangari is not alone.
Talk of the trees spreads over all of Africa,
like ripples in Lake Victoria.

More women hear the talk
and plant even more seedlings
in longer and longer rows.
The seedlings take root and grow tall—
until there are over 30 million trees
where there were none.

The umbrella of green in Kenya returns.

Women walk tall, their backs straight,
for now they can gather firewood closer to home.

The land is no longer barren.
Sweet potatoes, sugarcane, and maize
grow again in the rich, red earth.

The whole world hears of Wangari's trees
and of her army of women who planted them.

And if you were to climb to the very top
of Mount Kenya today, you would see
the millions of trees growing below you,

and the green Wangari brought back to Africa.

AUTHOR'S NOTE

Wangari Maathai was born in 1940 in Ihithe, a small village in the verdant, fertile land of Kenya. Brilliant in school, Wangari was awarded a Kennedy Scholarship to attend college in America, where she earned both a bachelor's and master's degree in the biological sciences. Wangari returned to Kenya to attend the University of Nairobi and became the first woman from East Africa to earn a Ph.D. She taught at the university and today is a member of Parliament in Kenya.

Wangari started Green Belt Movement Kenya in 1977 on World Environment Day by planting nine seedlings in her backyard. She was responding to the growing deforestation of her homeland. She saw many changes in daily life, especially among rural women. Some of these changes were lack of firewood, poor soil, erosion, and lack of clean drinking water. The desert was creeping closer, encroaching on the fields where crops and trees once flourished.

She enlisted local women to help her plant more indigenous trees. By 2004, thirty million trees had been planted, six thousand nurseries existed in Kenya, the income of eighty thousand people had been increased, and the movement had spread to thirty African countries—and beyond.

Wangari Maathai was awarded the Nobel Peace Prize in 2004 because of her contribution to world peace through the Green Belt Movement. In African tradition, a tree is a symbol of peace. So it was fitting that when notified of winning the award, one of Wangari's first acts was to plant a Nandi flame tree at the base of Mount Kenya. In her acceptance speech she said:

"We are called to assist the Earth to heal her wounds and in the process heal our own—indeed, to embrace the whole creation in all its diversity, beauty and wonder."